California
Bingo Book

COMPLETE BINGO GAME IN A BOOK

CALIFORNIA REPUBLIC

Written By Rebecca Stark
Educational Books 'n' Bingo

978-0-87386-498-5

Educational Books 'n' Bingo

Printed in the United States of America.

DIRECTIONS

INCLUDED:

List of Terms

Templates for Additional Terms and Clues

2 Clues per Term

30 Unique Bingo Cards

Markers

1. **Either cut apart the book or make copies of ALL the sheets. You might want to make an extra copy of the clue sheets to use for introduction and review. Keep the sheets in an envelope for easy reuse.**

2. Cut apart the call cards with terms and clues.

3. Pass out one bingo card per student. There are enough for a class of 30.

4. Pass out markers. You may cut apart the markers included in this book or use any other small items of your choice.

5. Decide whether or not you will require the entire card to be filled. Requiring the entire card to be filled provides a better review. However, if you have a short time to fill, you may prefer to have them do the just the border or some other format. Tell the class before you begin what is required.

6. There are 50 terms. Read the list before you begin. If there are any terms that have not been covered in class, you may want to read to the students the term and clues before you begin.

7. There is a blank space in the middle of each card. You can instruct the students to use it as a free space or you can write in answers to cover terms not included. Of course, in this case you would create your own clues. (Templates provided.)

8. Shuffle the cards and place them in a pile. Two or three clues are provided for each term. If you plan to play the game with the same group more than once, you might want to choose a different clue for each game. If not, you may choose to use more than one clue.

9. Be sure to keep the cards you have used for the present game in a separate pile. When a student calls, "Bingo," he or she will have to verify that the correct answers are on his or her card AND that the markers were placed in response to the proper questions. Pull out the cards that are on the student's card keeping them in the order they were used in the game. Read each clue as it was given and ask the student to identify the correct answer from his or her card.

10. If the student has the correct answers on the card AND has shown that they were marked in response to the *correct questions,* then that student is the winner and the game is over. If the student does not have the correct answers on the card OR he or she marked the answers in response to *the wrong questions,* then the game continues until there is a proper winner.

11. If you want to play again, reshuffle the cards and begin again.

Have fun!

TERMS INCLUDED

Borders	Motto
Juan Rodriguez Cabrillo	Native American
California Trail	Richard M. Nixon
Climate	Oakland
Coachella Valley	Point(s)
Compromise of 1850	Populous
County(-ies)	Presidios
Executive Branch	Pueblos
Fault	Ranchos
Flag	Redwood(s)
John C. Frémont	Ronald Reagan
Geographic Regions	Sally Ride
Gold Rush	River
Golden State	Sacramento
Golden Gate Bridge	San Diego
Gray Whale(s)	San Francisco
Industry (-ies)	San Jose
Judicial Branch	Sequoia National Park
Lake(s)	Sierra Nevada
Legislative Branch	Silicon Valley
Los Angeles	Transcontinental Railroad
Mexican-American War	Union
Missions	Earl Warren
Mojave Desert	Wine (-eries)
Monterey	Yosemite

California Bingo

Additional Terms

Choose as many additional terms as you would like and write them in the squares. Repeat each as desired.

Cut out the squares and randomly distribute them to the class.

Instruct the students to place their square on the center space of their card.

California Bingo

© **Barbara M. Peller**

Clues for Additional Terms

Write three clues for each of your additional terms.

1. _____ 2. 3.	1. _____ 2. 3.
1. _____ 2. 3.	1. _____ 2. 3.
1. _____ 2. 3.	1. _____ 2. 3.

Borders 1. Oregon, Nevada, Arizona and Mexico are the state's land ___. 2. The Pacific Ocean ___ California to the west.	**Juan Rodriguez Cabrillo** 1. This Portuguese explorer explored the west coast of North America for Spain. 2. ___ was the first European explorer to navigate the coast of California.
California Trail 1.The ___ was an overland wagon trail of about 2,000 miles from Missouri River towns to what is now the state of California. 2. Starting in late 1848 more than 250,000 people, many of them gold-seekers, went by way of the ___ to California.	**Climate** 1. The ___ of California varies widely, from arid to subarctic, depending on latitude, elevation, and nearness to the coast. 2. Coastal and southern parts of the state have a Mediterranean ___, with somewhat rainy winters and dry summers. Farther inland there are colder winters and hotter summers.
Coachella Valley 1. The desert resort cities of Palm Springs and Palm Desert lie in the ___. 2. This agricultural and recreational desert valley in southern California is east of Riverside and San Bernardino.	**Compromise of 1850** 1. Drafted by Henry Clay of Kentucky, the ___ dealt with the status of territories acquired as a result of the Mexican-American War. 2. The ___ included the approval of California's application for admission to the Union as a free state.
County(-ies) 1. There are 58 ___ in the state of California. San Francisco is the only consolidated city–___ in the state. 2. Each ___ has a board of supervisors.	**Executive Branch** 1. The governor is head of the ___ of government. The present-day governor is [fill in]. 2. The ___ comprises the governor, lieutenant governor, secretary of state, state controller, state treasurer, state attorney general, state insurance commissioner and state superin-tendent of public instruction as well as many agencies.
Fault 1. A ___ is a crack in the earth's crust resulting from the displacement of one side with respect to the other. 2. California has many earthquakes because the San Andreas ___ runs through the state.	**Flag** 1. The field of the state ___ is white with a broad red stripe at the bottom. 2. The state ___ has a red star, a bear, and the words "CALIFORNIA REPUBLIC" in the white field.

John C. Frémont

1. ___ organized the first California Volunteer Militia and was one of the first two U.S. senators elected from California in 1850.
2. This explorer and trailblazer is sometimes called The Great Pathfinder.

Geographic Regions

1. The 4 coastal ___ of California include Bay Area, Central Coast, Coastal North and Southern California Coastal.
2. The 5 inland ___ of California include Central Valley North, Central Valley South, Mountain North, Mountain South and Southern California Inland.

Gold Rush

1. The California ___ began in 1848 when gold was found by James W. Marshall at Sutter's Mill in Coloma, California.
2. The ___ brought about 300,000 people to California from the rest of the United States and abroad.

Golden State

1. The ___ became the official state nickname in 1968.
2. The nickname ___ might refer to the discovery of gold in the state; it might also refer to the fields of yellow poppies that bloom in the spring.

Golden Gate Bridge

1. This beautiful suspension bridge connects the city of San Francisco to Marin County.
2. The ___ is named for the strait that connects San Francisco Bay to the Pacific Ocean.

Gray Whale(s)

1. The California ___ is the state marine mammal.
2. California ___ migrate from the western Bering Sea to Baja California and back again. These migrations draw thousands of sightseers to the coast every year.

Industry (-ies)

1. California is a leading industrial state. Machinery, agricultural products, food processing, and aerospace technology are among the many important ___.
2. The tourism ___ is very important to the state's economy.

Judicial Branch

1. The ___ interprets what our laws mean and makes decisions about the laws and those who break them.
2. The ___ is made up of several courts, the highest of which is the state Supreme Court.

Lake(s)

1. There are more than 3,000 named ___ in California. The largest in terms of area covered is the Salton Sea; however, it is very shallow.
2. ___ Tahoe, which is on the California-Nevada border, is the largest in terms of volume.

Legislative Branch

1. The state ___ comprises the California State Assembly and the California State Senate.
2. The ___ makes the laws.

California Bingo

Los Angeles 1. ___ is the second most populous city in the United States. New York City is the most populous. 2. Hollywood, a district of ___, is the historical center of movie studios.	**Mexican-American War** 1. The ___ took place from 1846 to 1848. 2. The Treaty of Guadalupe Hidalgo ended the ___. Part of that treaty was the Mexican Cession of the territories of Alta California and New Mexico to the U.S.
Missions 1. The Spanish established ___ to spread the Christian faith among the local Native Americans. 2. These religious and military outposts were established by Spanish Catholics of the Franciscan Order between 1769 and 1823.	**Mojave Desert** 1. The ___ is an area of transition from the hot Sonoran Desert to the cooler, higher Great Basin. 2. The ___'s boundaries are generally defined by the presence of Joshua trees.
Monterey 1. ___ was established in 1770 by Father Junípero Serra and explorer Gaspar de Portolà; it was the capital of Alta California. 2. The ___ Peninsula comprises ___, Carmel, Pacific Grove, and some unincorporated areas, including Pebble Beach.	**Motto** 1. The state ___ of California is "Eureka...I have found it!" It appears on the state seal. 2. The state ___ refers to the discovery of gold in the state.
Native American 1. California has the largest number of distinct ___ tribes of any state. 2. ___ tribes on the eastern border with Nevada are classified as Great Basin tribes; some on the Oregon border are classified as Plateau tribes.	**Richard M. Nixon** 1. This Californian ___ was the 37th President of the United States. 2. ___ resigned as President following what became known as the Watergate Scandal.
Oakland 1. This city is connected to San Francisco by the Bay Bridge. 2. Lake Merritt, a large tidal lagoon, lies east of downtown ___. It was the nation's first official wildlife refuge.	**Point(s)** 1. California contains both the highest and lowest ___ in the contiguous United States. Mount McKinley in Alaska is higher. 2. Mount Whitney is the highest ___ in California, and Death Valley is the lowest.

Populous 1. California is the most ___ state in the Union. 2. Three of the top ten most ___ cities in the nation are in California: Los Angeles, San Diego, and San Jose. San Francisco is the fourteenth most ___.	**Presidios** 1. ___ were fortresses established in the southwestern United States by the Spanish. 2. The ___ of San Francisco served as an army post for three nations: Spain, Mexico and the United States.
Pueblos 1. ___ were farming communities built close to the missions and settled by people from Mexico. 2. The ___ differed from other Spanish settlements because they were not run by priests or soldiers.	**Ranchos** 1. The Spanish and later the Mexican government encouraged settlement of territory now known as California by the establishment of large land grants, called ___. 2. Pasadena, Huntington Beach, San Clemente, Oakland, and other cities are on land that was once part of Spanish land grants, called ___.
Redwood(s) 1. Located in southwestern Marin County, Muir Woods is an old-growth coastal ___ forest. 2. The California ___ is the official state tree. Giant ___ trees are the tallest trees in the world.	**Ronald Reagan** 1. He was the 33rd governor of California and the 40th President of the United States. 2. A few years before becoming governor of the state, he served as President of the Screen Actors Guild.
Sally Ride 1. This astronaut was born in Encino, which is part of Los Angeles, California. 2. In 1983 ___ became the first American woman to enter space.	**River** 1. The Colorado ___ separates Arizona and California; it is the principal river of the southwestern United States. 2. The longest ___ entirely within California is the Sacramento ___.
Sacramento 1. ___ is the capital of California. 2. ___ is located at the confluence of the Sacramento and American rivers in the northern portion of the Central Valley.	**San Diego** 1. ___ is the second largest city in California; it is located on the Pacific coast, adjacent to the Mexican border. 2. Balboa Park and the zoo are popular tourist destinations of this city.
California Bingo	© Barbara M. Peller

San Francisco 1. Famous landmarks of ___ include the Golden Gate Bridge, Alcatraz Island, cable cars and streetcars, Coit Tower, and Chinatown. 2. ___ is the fourth most populous city in California after Los Angeles, San Diego and San Jose, but it is the most densely populated.	**San Jose** 1. ___ served as the first state capital when California gained statehood in 1850. 2. ___ is the third most populous city in California. It is in the Santa Clara Valley.
Sequoia National Park 1. ___ and Kings Canyon National Park lie side by side in the southern Sierra Nevada, east of the San Joaquin Valley. 2. ___ is famous for its giant trees. It also contains Mount Whitney, the highest point in the contiguous 48 United States. (*contiguous:* touching or connected throughout in an unbroken sequence)	**Sierra Nevada** 1. Yosemite, Sequoia, Kings Canyon national parks are all in the ___. 2. The ___ is a mountain range between the California Central Valley and the Basin and Range Province.
Silicon Valley 1. The southern part of the San Francisco Bay Area is nicknamed ___. 2. The nickname ___ has come to refer to all the high-tech businesses in the area.	**Transcontinental Railroad** 1. Oakland was selected as the western terminus of the ___. 2. The ___ was built by the Central Pacific Railroad of California and the Union Pacific Railroad.
Union 1. California was admitted to the ___ on September 9, 1850. It became the 31st state. 2. California entered the ___ as a free state by the Compromise of 1850.	**Earl Warren** 1. ___ was elected governor of California three times before becoming the 14th chief justice of the United States. 2. Some of the decisions of the Court when he was chief justice ended school segregation.
Wine (-eries) 1. There are more than 1,200 ___ in the state. The Central Valley is California's largest ___ region. 2 Two well-known areas for ___ are Napa and Sonoma Valley.	**Yosemite** 1. ___ National Park, one of the first wilderness parks in the nation, is best known for its waterfalls. ___ Falls is the tallest waterfall in North America. 2. El Capitan is a vertical rock formation in ___. It means "the chief" in Spanish; it is the largest piece of granite in North America.
California Bingo	© **Barbara M. Peller**

California Bingo

River	Borders	California Trail	Judicial Branch	Coachella Valley
Gray Whale(s)	Juan Rodriguez Cabrillo	Union	Point(s)	San Diego
Transcontinental Railroad	Oakland		Redwood(s)	Earl Warren
Silicon Valley	Wine (-eries)	Sierra Nevada	Richard M. Nixon	Presidios
Ranchos	Mexican-American War	Gold Rush	San Jose	Monterey

California Bingo

Silicon Valley	Transcontinental Railroad	Mojave Desert	Sacramento	Native American
Presidios	Golden State	Executive Branch	Wine (-eries)	Pueblos
Flag	Mexican-American War		Missions	Sierra Nevada
Ronald Reagan	Sally Ride	Oakland	Yosemite	Coachella Valley
San Diego	Union	Gold Rush	Gray Whale(s)	San Jose

California Bingo

Mexican-American War	Sierra Nevada	Golden State	Richard M. Nixon	Transcontinental Railroad
Presidios	Juan Rodriguez Cabrillo	Fault	Borders	Los Angeles
Wine (-eries)	Union		Pueblos	Climate
Oakland	Flag	Ranchos	Ronald Reagan	Mojave Desert
San Jose	John C. Frémont	Gold Rush	Yosemite	Native American

California Bingo: Card No. 3

California Bingo

Oakland	Pueblos	California Trail	John C. Frémont	Native American
Populous	County(-ies)	Borders	Sacramento	Transcontinental Railroad
Redwood(s)	Ronald Reagan		Monterey	Judicial Branch
Sierra Nevada	Juan Rodriguez Cabrillo	Union	Gold Rush	Executive Branch
Lake(s)	San Diego	Compromise of 1850	San Jose	Earl Warren

California Bingo

San Diego	Coachella Valley	Wine (-eries)	Executive Branch	John C. Frémont
Populous	Sierra Nevada	Fault	Missions	Juan Rodriguez Cabrillo
California Trail	Earl Warren		Point(s)	Legislative Branch
Monterey	Native American	River	Yosemite	Geographic Regions
Golden State	Gold Rush	Transcontinental Railroad	Oakland	Redwood(s)

California Bingo: Card No. 5

California Bingo

Climate	Pueblos	Mojave Desert	Native American	Earl Warren
Richard M. Nixon	Wine (-eries)	Geographic Regions	Borders	Transcontinental Railroad
Sacramento	Lake(s)		County(-ies)	Missions
Gold Rush	Ranchos	Yosemite	Compromise of 1850	California Trail
Presidios	Executive Branch	River	Redwood(s)	Golden Gate Bridge

California Bingo: Card No. 6

California Bingo

River	Pueblos	Legislative Branch	Sierra Nevada	Golden State
Presidios	Native American	Mexican-American War	Juan Rodriguez Cabrillo	Populous
Earl Warren	Judicial Branch		Missions	County(-ies)
Oakland	Ronald Reagan	Fault	Silicon Valley	Flag
Gold Rush	John C. Frémont	Yosemite	Compromise of 1850	Climate

California Bingo: Card No. 7

California Bingo

Redwood(s)	Pueblos	Industry (-ies)	Richard M. Nixon	County(-ies)
Populous	California Trail	Sacramento	Earl Warren	Executive Branch
Golden Gate Bridge	John C. Frémont		Native American	Coachella Valley
San Jose	Oakland	Silicon Valley	Lake(s)	Ronald Reagan
Union	Gold Rush	Compromise of 1850	Wine (-eries)	Presidios

California Bingo: Card No. 8

California Bingo

Missions	Golden State	Mexican-American War	Golden Gate Bridge	John C. Frémont
Lake(s)	Native American	Redwood(s)	Wine (-eries)	Pueblos
Los Angeles	River		Juan Rodriguez Cabrillo	Industry (-ies)
Geographic Regions	Coachella Valley	Ranchos	Point(s)	Legislative Branch
Ronald Reagan	Yosemite	Fault	Silicon Valley	Monterey

California Bingo: Card No. 9

California Bingo

Silicon Valley	Richard M. Nixon	County(-ies)	Sacramento	Golden Gate Bridge
Earl Warren	Executive Branch	Borders	Juan Rodriguez Cabrillo	Native American
John C. Frémont	Pueblos		Judicial Branch	Flag
Ranchos	Monterey	Geographic Regions	Yosemite	Los Angeles
Fault	Presidios	Mojave Desert	San Diego	Redwood(s)

California Bingo: Card No. 10

California Bingo

Climate	Pueblos	Wine (-eries)	Geographic Regions	Presidios
Industry (-ies)	Los Angeles	Point(s)	Missions	Borders
Populous	Native American		Mojave Desert	Mexican-American War
Fault	Transcontinental Railroad	Yosemite	John C. Frémont	Silicon Valley
Lake(s)	Gold Rush	River	Compromise of 1850	Golden State

California Bingo

Golden State	Coachella Valley	Los Angeles	Richard M. Nixon	Missions
Mexican-American War	Presidios	California Trail	Compromise of 1850	Juan Rodriguez Cabrillo
River	Legislative Branch		Earl Warren	Sacramento
Gold Rush	Ronald Reagan	Native American	Silicon Valley	Populous
Pueblos	Industry (-ies)	John C. Frémont	Lake(s)	Executive Branch

California Bingo

Geographic Regions	Coachella Valley	Climate	Los Angeles	Earl Warren
California Trail	Industry (-ies)	Native American	Missions	Flag
Richard M. Nixon	Executive Branch		Mexican-American War	Legislative Branch
Redwood(s)	Yosemite	County(-ies)	John C. Frémont	Silicon Valley
Gold Rush	Monterey	Compromise of 1850	River	Point(s)

California Bingo

Gray Whale(s)	Native American	Wine (-eries)	Missions	Lake(s)
Executive Branch	River	Los Angeles	Juan Rodriguez Cabrillo	Pueblos
Geographic Regions	Judicial Branch		Mojave Desert	Fault
Monterey	Yosemite	John C. Frémont	County(-ies)	Climate
Gold Rush	Sacramento	Flag	Presidios	Redwood(s)

California Bingo

Point(s)	Missions	Wine (-eries)	Golden State	Richard M. Nixon
Climate	Mojave Desert	Borders	California Trail	Lake(s)
Earl Warren	River		Transcontinental Railroad	Pueblos
Gold Rush	Los Angeles	Industry (-ies)	Yosemite	Geographic Regions
Presidios	Ronald Reagan	Compromise of 1850	Golden Gate Bridge	Mexican-American War

California Bingo

County(-ies)	Los Angeles	Industry (-ies)	Golden Gate Bridge	Sally Ride
Sacramento	Flag	Legislative Branch	Populous	Judicial Branch
Geographic Regions	Coachella Valley		Earl Warren	Mexican-American War
Oakland	Executive Branch	Gold Rush	Point(s)	Silicon Valley
Lake(s)	Sequoia National Park	Compromise of 1850	Ronald Reagan	Pueblos

California Bingo: Card No. 16

California Bingo

Fault	San Francisco	Motto	Los Angeles	Gray Whale(s)
Point(s)	Lake(s)	Yosemite	Judicial Branch	Legislative Branch
Missions	Redwood(s)		Sequoia National Park	Industry (-ies)
Monterey	Presidios	Silicon Valley	Wine (-eries)	Flag
Ranchos	Geographic Regions	Golden State	Richard M. Nixon	Coachella Valley

California Bingo

Golden Gate Bridge	John C. Frémont	Executive Branch	Geographic Regions	Sacramento
Pueblos	Fault	Ranchos	Earl Warren	Lake(s)
Missions	Flag		Motto	California Trail
Coachella Valley	Borders	Yosemite	Silicon Valley	Mojave Desert
Sequoia National Park	Los Angeles	Wine (-eries)	San Francisco	Climate

California Bingo: Card No. 18

California Bingo

Earl Warren	Climate	Los Angeles	Industry (-ies)	Silicon Valley
Point(s)	Richard M. Nixon	Pueblos	Golden State	Judicial Branch
San Francisco	John C. Frémont		Juan Rodriguez Cabrillo	Transcontinental Railroad
Mojave Desert	Sequoia National Park	Ranchos	Ronald Reagan	Motto
California Trail	Sally Ride	Presidios	Redwood(s)	Compromise of 1850

California Bingo: Card No. 19

California Bingo

Gray Whale(s)	San Francisco	Richard M. Nixon	Los Angeles	Compromise of 1850
Executive Branch	Mexican-American War	Populous	Ranchos	Sacramento
Coachella Valley	Legislative Branch		Oakland	Borders
San Diego	Union	San Jose	Ronald Reagan	Sequoia National Park
Sierra Nevada	Redwood(s)	Sally Ride	Silicon Valley	Motto

California Bingo

Point(s)	Climate	Populous	Los Angeles	San Diego
Coachella Valley	Motto	County(-ies)	Industry (-ies)	River
Flag	Presidios		San Francisco	Wine (-eries)
Ranchos	Golden State	Sequoia National Park	Monterey	Redwood(s)
Oakland	Sally Ride	Compromise of 1850	Fault	Ronald Reagan

California Bingo

Golden Gate Bridge	Mojave Desert	Motto	California Trail	Geographic Regions
Sacramento	Richard M. Nixon	Transcontinental Railroad	Industry (-ies)	Juan Rodriguez Cabrillo
Executive Branch	Judicial Branch		River	Legislative Branch
Sequoia National Park	Monterey	Ronald Reagan	Borders	Populous
Sally Ride	Fault	San Francisco	Flag	San Diego

California Bingo

County(-ies)	San Francisco	Golden State	California Trail	Compromise of 1850
Climate	Gray Whale(s)	Presidios	Point(s)	Borders
Mojave Desert	Geographic Regions		San Jose	River
Flag	Sally Ride	Sequoia National Park	Fault	Ronald Reagan
San Diego	Union	Redwood(s)	Ranchos	Motto

California Bingo

County(-ies)	Redwood(s)	Gray Whale(s)	San Francisco	Industry (-ies)
Motto	Compromise of 1850	Populous	Sacramento	River
Legislative Branch	Golden Gate Bridge		Geographic Regions	Flag
San Diego	San Jose	Sequoia National Park	Fault	Coachella Valley
Sierra Nevada	Oakland	Sally Ride	Richard M. Nixon	Union

California Bingo

Oakland	Populous	San Francisco	Wine (-eries)	Motto
Borders	Coachella Valley	Point(s)	County(-ies)	Juan Rodriguez Cabrillo
Monterey	Industry (-ies)		San Jose	Sequoia National Park
Transcontinental Railroad	San Diego	Union	Sally Ride	Judicial Branch
Compromise of 1850	Gray Whale(s)	Executive Branch	Lake(s)	Sierra Nevada

California Bingo

Motto	San Francisco	Mojave Desert	Sacramento	Golden Gate Bridge
Ranchos	Richard M. Nixon	Industry (-ies)	Gray Whale(s)	County(-ies)
Monterey	San Jose		Judicial Branch	Oakland
Fault	California Trail	San Diego	Sally Ride	Sequoia National Park
Legislative Branch	Lake(s)	Wine (-eries)	Union	Sierra Nevada

California Bingo: Card No. 26

California Bingo

Mojave Desert	Executive Branch	San Francisco	Gray Whale(s)	Mexican-American War
San Diego	San Jose	Point(s)	Sequoia National Park	Juan Rodriguez Cabrillo
Yosemite	Union		Sally Ride	Oakland
Golden Gate Bridge	Climate	Populous	Sierra Nevada	Borders
Lake(s)	Judicial Branch	Motto	Transcontinental Railroad	Legislative Branch

California Bingo: Card No. 27

California Bingo

Mojave Desert	Gray Whale(s)	Transcontinental Railroad	San Francisco	County(-ies)
Mexican-American War	Motto	San Jose	Sacramento	Judicial Branch
Union	Flag		Legislative Branch	Ranchos
Silicon Valley	Golden Gate Bridge	Presidios	Sally Ride	Sequoia National Park
California Trail	Missions	Lake(s)	Sierra Nevada	San Diego

California Bingo: Card No. 28

California Bingo

Motto	Gray Whale(s)	Golden Gate Bridge	Point(s)	Missions
Ronald Reagan	Ranchos	Populous	Legislative Branch	Transcontinental Railroad
Monterey	San Jose		Juan Rodriguez Cabrillo	San Francisco
Mexican-American War	San Diego	Native American	Sally Ride	Sequoia National Park
County(-ies)	Industry (-ies)	Sierra Nevada	Climate	Union

California Bingo: Card No. 29

California Bingo

John C. Frémont	San Francisco	Sacramento	Missions	Sequoia National Park
Borders	Gray Whale(s)	Mojave Desert	Judicial Branch	Juan Rodriguez Cabrillo
Monterey	Geographic Regions		Legislative Branch	Populous
Sierra Nevada	Climate	California Trail	Sally Ride	San Jose
San Diego	Earl Warren	Union	Motto	Transcontinental Railroad

California Bingo: Card No. 30

www.ingramcontent.com/pod-product-compliance
Lightning Source LLC
LaVergne TN
LVHW061337060426
835511LV00014B/1965